What Can I Make Today?

I Can Make a
Truck

Joanna Issa

Chicago, Illinois

© 2015 Heinemann Library, an imprint of Capstone
Global Library, LLC
Chicago, Illinois

To contact Capstone Global Library please
call 800-747-4992, or visit our web site:
www.capstonepub.com

Edited by Penny West
Designed by Philippa Jenkins
Picture research by Elizabeth Alexander
Originated by Capstone Global Library Ltd
Production by Victoria Fitzgerald
Printed and bound in China by Leo Paper Group

18 17 16 15 14
10 9 8 7 6 5 4 3 2 1

Library of Congress Cataloging-in-Publication Data
Issa, Joanna, author.
  I can make a truck / Joanna Issa.
     pages cm.—(What can I make today?)
  Summary: "Using simple text and step-by-step
instructions alongside clear, labeled photographs,
this book shows how to make a cool truck out of
cardboard boxes and other household materials"—
Provided by publisher.
  Includes bibliographical references and index.
  ISBN 978-1-4846-0462-5 (hb)
  1. Paper work—Juvenile literature. 2. Handicraft—
Juvenile literature. 3. Trucks in art—Juvenile
literature. I. Title.

TT870.I865 2015
745.5—dc23   2013039813

Acknowledgments
We would like to thank Capstone Publishers/
© Karon Dubke for permission to reproduce
photographs.

Cover photograph reproduced with permission of
Capstone Publishers/ © Karon Dubke.

We would like to thank Philippa Jenkins for her
invaluable help in the preparation of this book.

Every effort has been made to contact copyright
holders of any material reproduced in this book.
Any omissions will be rectified in subsequent
printings if notice is given to the publisher.

Disclaimer
All the Internet addresses (URLs) given in this
book were valid at the time of going to press.
However, due to the dynamic nature of the
Internet, some addresses may have changed,
or sites may have changed or ceased to exist
since publication. While the author and publisher
regret any inconvenience this may cause readers,
no responsibility for any such changes can be
accepted by either the author or the publisher.

Contents

What Do I Need to
    Make a Truck? 4

Make the Trailer 6

Make the Cab 9

Make the Axles 15

Make the Wheels 18

What Can You Make Today? 22

Picture Glossary 23

Find Out More 24

Some words are shown in bold,
like this. You can find them in
the glossary on page 23.

What Do I Need to Make a Truck?

To make the cab and **trailer**, you will need a large box, a small box that's the same width as the large box, card stock, a brad, double-sided tape, masking tape, a pencil, and scissors.

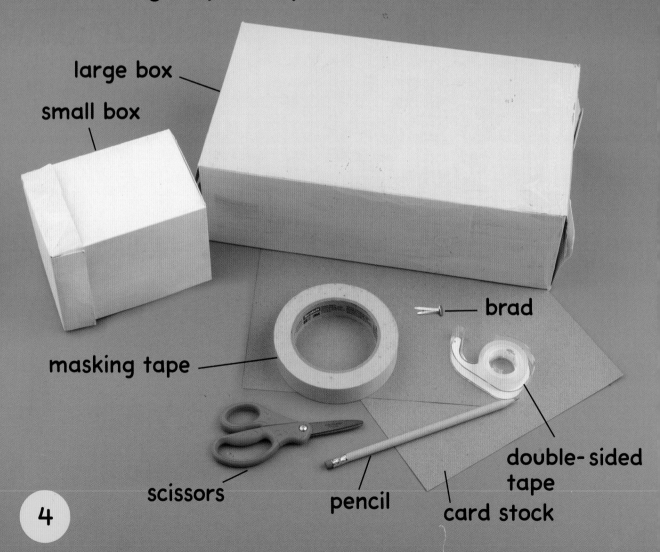

large box

small box

brad

masking tape

scissors

pencil

card stock

double-sided tape

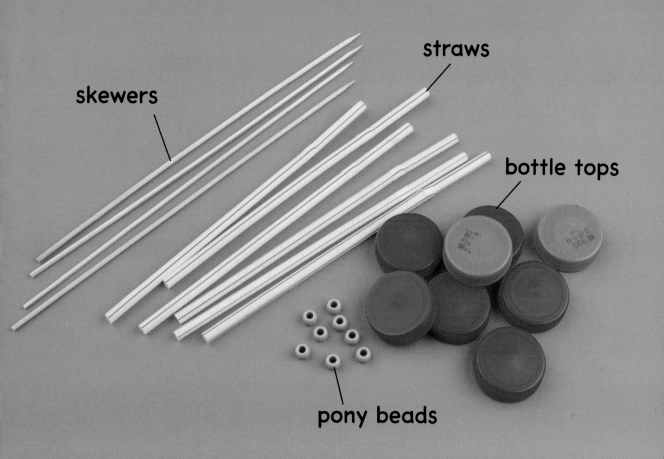

skewers

straws

bottle tops

pony beads

To make the wheels and **axles**, you will need four **skewers**, eight pony beads with a large enough hole for a skewer, six straws, and eight bottle tops.

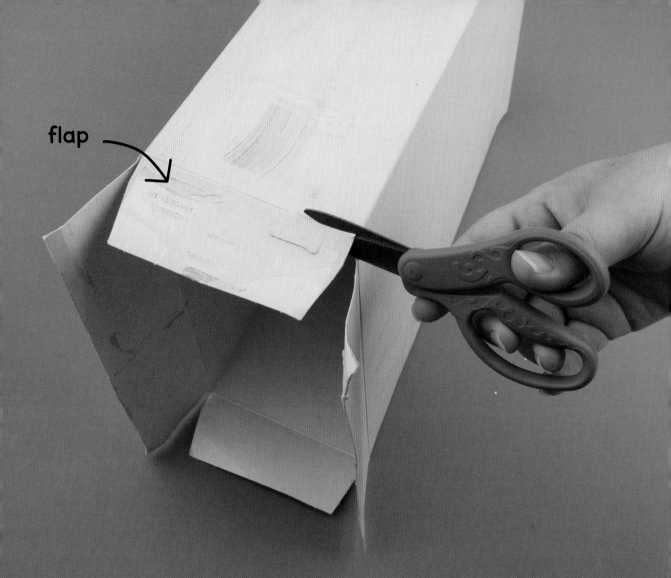

flap

Make the Trailer

Use the large box to make the **trailer**. To make the trailer **ramp**, open one end of the large box and cut off the top flap.

Cut a rectangle of card stock so it is
the same width and height as the end
of the large box. Stick it to the bottom
flap of the box with masking tape.

7

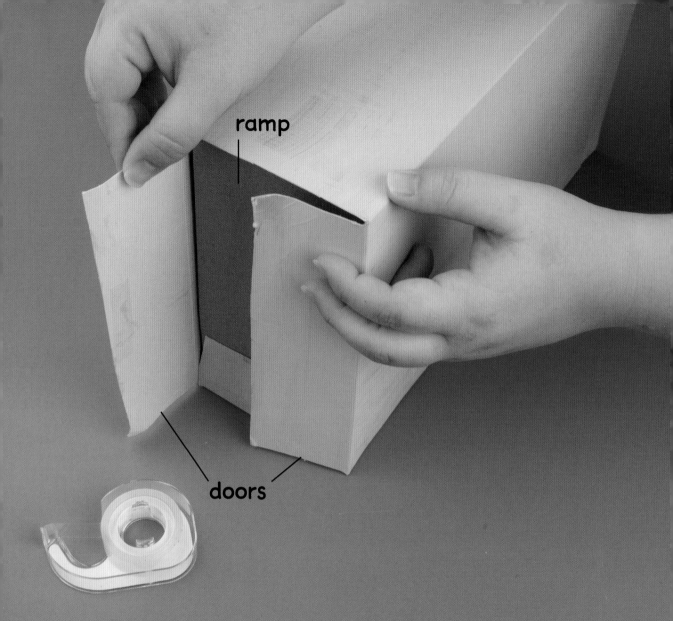

ramp

doors

To close the doors, push the **ramp** up, then use double-sided tape to secure the doors.

Make the Cab

Use the small box to make the cab. To make the front window, draw a rectangle on one of the wide sides of the box. Next, make the side windows. Draw a square on each of the short sides of the box. Then ask an adult to help you cut out the shapes.

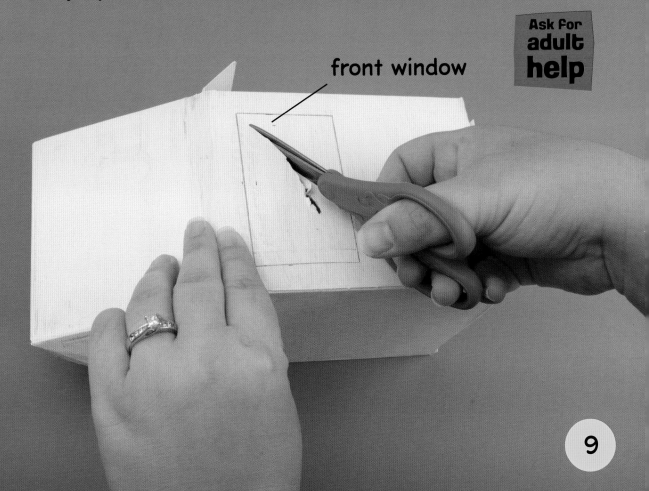

Ask for **adult help**

front window

Lift the lid of the small box to make the roof of the cab.

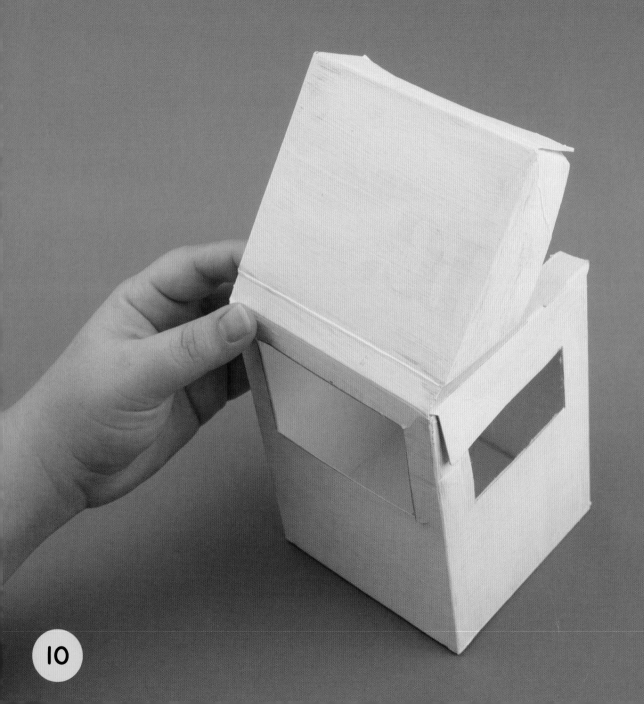

To attach the cab to the **trailer**, cut a rectangle from card stock. It should be 4 inches (10 centimeters) longer than the cab. Stick double-sided tape to one end of the rectangle.

Ask for **adult help**

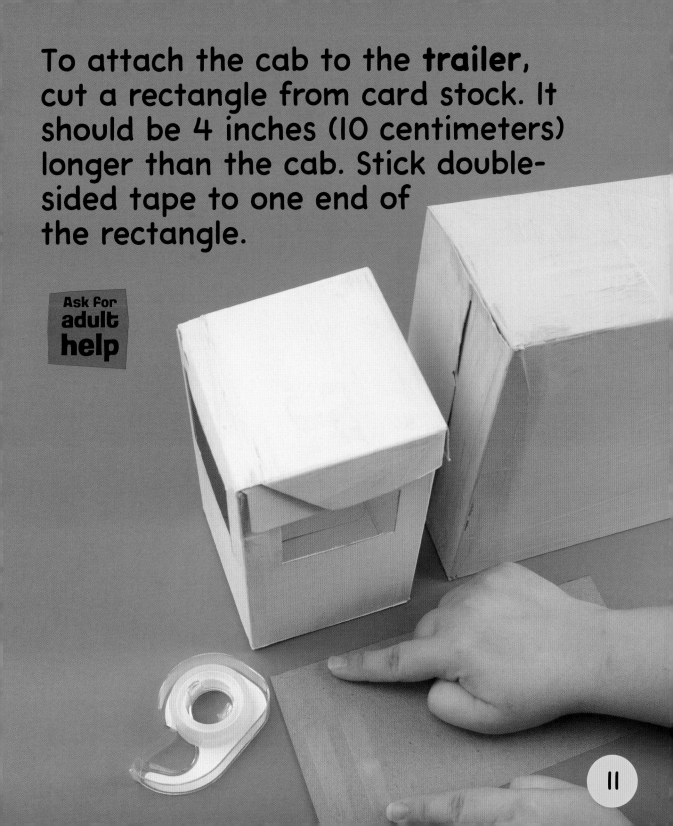

Stick the cab onto the card stock.

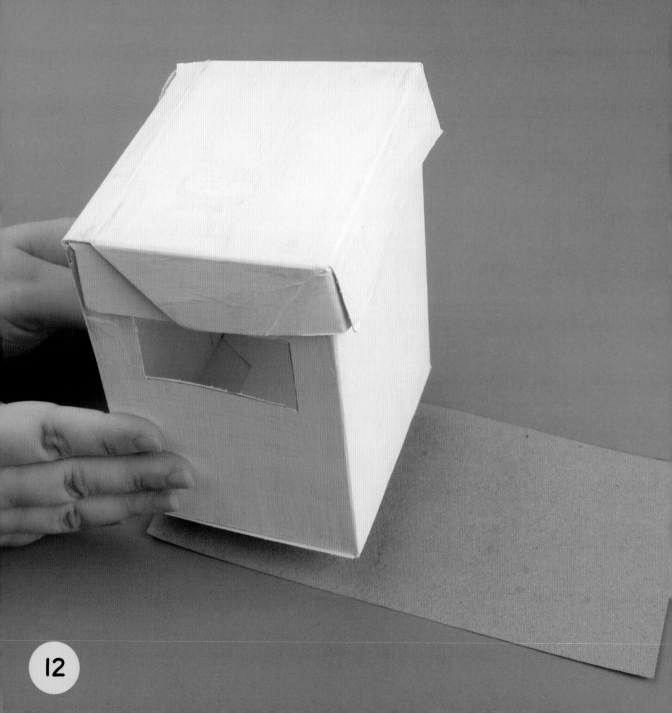

Make a hole in the end of the card stock with the brad.

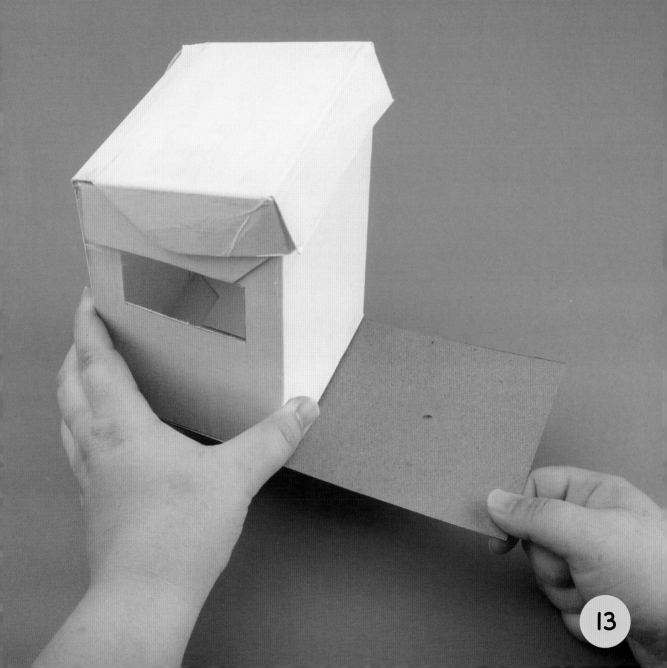

Make a hole in the **trailer** with the brad. Leave a small space between the cab and the trailer. Push a brad through the holes to attach the trailer to the card stock.

Make the Axles

Cut four straws a little wider than the truck. Tape three straws underneath the trailer and one straw underneath the cab.

Cut the wooden **skewers** so they are 1 inch (2 centimeters) longer than the straws.

Ask for
adult help

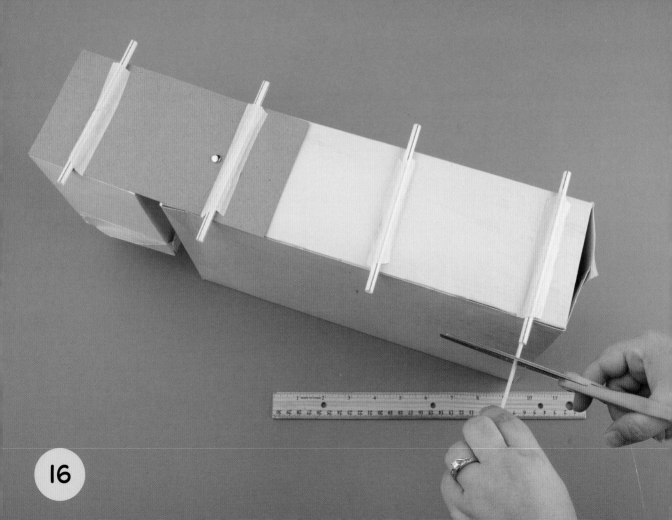

Push the skewers inside the straws.

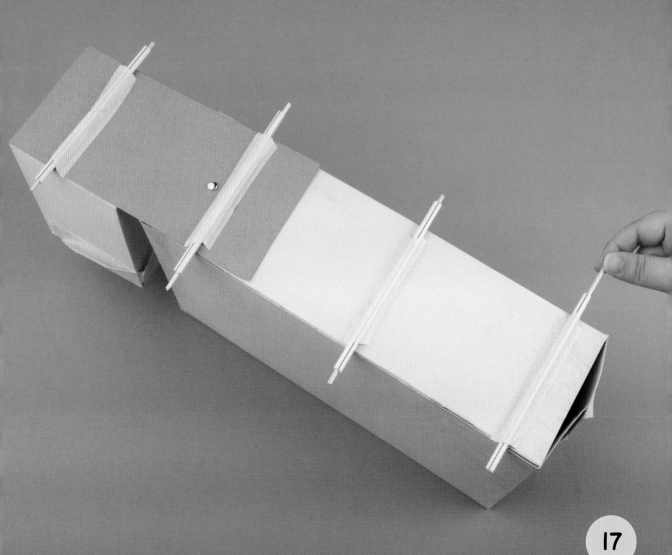

Make the Wheels

Ask an adult to make a hole in each bottle top. Each hole should be big enough to fit onto a **skewer**.

Push a bottle top onto the end of each wooden skewer. Stick a small piece of double-sided tape around the end of the skewer.

Push the pony bead on to hold it in place. Do this for all the wheels.

Stick a straw to each side of the cab.
You have finished your truck! You
can decorate it with paint or colored
paper if you like.

What Can You Make Today?

You could make a truck and **trailer** as a gift for Father's Day or a birthday present.

Picture Glossary

axle long rod that the wheels are attached to

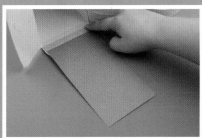

ramp flat part of the trailer that can be lowered or raised

skewer thin stick used to hold pieces of food together

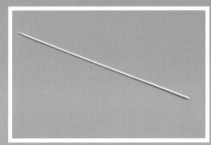

trailer part of the truck that is towed by the cab

Find Out More

Books

Bull, Jane. *Make It!* New York: Dorling Kindersley, 2013.

Smith, Sian. *Machines on the Road.* Chicago: Raintree, 2013.

Web sites

Facthound offers a safe, fun way to find Internet sites related to this book. All of the sites on Facthound have been researched by our staff.

Here's all you do:
Visit www.facthound.com
Type in this code: 9781484604625

Index

axles 5, 15–17, 23
bottle tops 5, 18, 19
cab 4, 9–10, 11, 12, 14, 15
ramp 6–7, 8, 23

skewers 5, 16–17, 19, 23
straws 5, 15, 17, 21
trailer 4, 6–8, 11, 14, 15, 22, 23
wheels 5, 18–20